WHEN I'M AN

OLD COOT

ROY ENGLISH

WHEN I AM AN
OLD COOT

WITTICISMS

FOR PEOPLE WHO
REFUSE
TO GROW OLD
GRACEFULLY

➔

GIBBS SMITH
TO ENRICH AND INSPIRE HUMANKIND
Salt Lake City | Charleston | Santa Fe | Santa Barbara

Revised Edition
13 12   20 19 18 17 16 15 14 13 12 11 10 9 8 7 6 5

Text copyright © 1995 by Roy English
Flip cartoon illustrations by Steve Egan, © 1995 by Gibbs Smith,
Publisher

All rights reserved. No part of this book may be reproduced
by any means whatsoever without written permission from the
publisher, except brief portions quoted for purpose of review.

Published by
Gibbs Smith
P.O. Box 667
Layton, Utah 84041

1.800.835.4993 orders
www.gibbs-smith.com

Design by Black Eye Design
Printed and bound in the U.S.A.
Gibbs Smith books are printed on either recycled, 100 percent post-
consumer waste, FSC-certified papers or on paper produced from a
100 percent certified sustainable forest-controlled wood source.

Library of Congress Cataloging-in-Publication Data

English, Roy, 1943-
   When I am an old coot : witticisms for people who refuse to grow
old gracefully / Roy English. – 1st ed.
      p. cm.
   ISBN-13: 978-1-4236-0708-3
   ISBN-10: 1-4236-0708-2
   1. American wit and humor. I. Title.
   PN6162.E536 2009
   818'.5402—dc22

                                        2009018312

ISBN 13: 978-0-87905-695-7 (first edition)
ISBN 10: 0-87905-695-9 (first edition)

**TO OLD
COOTS
and free
spirits-**

**long may
they dance.**

When I am an old coot . . .

I will wear funny hats and loud ties, flowered underwear and bright yellow suspenders. I will break all the silly, proper rules and be a kid again.

I will teach young children the joys of blowing Jell-O on their little friends.

When I am an old coot . . .

I WILL PIERCE MY EAR AND WEAR A PICO PERCH IN CASE SOMEONE WANTS TO GO FISHING.

I will carry
my own trail
mix of salted
peanuts, Junior
Mints, candy
corn, and
Rolaids.

When I am an old coot . . .

I will perform my civic duty
by making sure all the residents at
The Home are registered to vote.

I will, of course, collect a small
poll tax for my trouble.

I WILL RIDE
A HARLEY-
DAVIDSON HOG
IN FUNERAL
PROCESSIONS
OF OLD GOLFING
BUDDIES AND
DESERVING
FRIENDS.

When I am an old coot . . .

I WILL MAKE A WILL
and donate my bones to the
Museum of Archaeology to be
exhibited as a "Fartasaurus Rex."

I will carry
my sleeping
bag to doctor
appointments
and nap on the
floor in the
waiting room.

When I am an old coot . . .

I will open
a restaurant
featuring
low-fat, no-salt,
low-cholesterol
foods. I
will hire
healthy young
waitresses and
call the place
"Cooters."

I WILL GO TO
THE DAIRY
QUEEN AND DIP
MY DENTURES
IN THE HOT
FUDGE WHEN
THE WAITRESS
ISN'T LOOKING.

I will trick
my forgetful
friends at
The Home by
giving myself a
birthday party
several times
a year and
asking them
to bring gifts.

I will go to a country western
nightclub and scatter the
line dancers with my personal version
OF THE "POOT SCOOTIN' BOOGIE."

When I am an old coot . . .

I will rent a limo for the day and show
up at busy offices all over town,

introduce myself as the new owner,
and give everyone the day off.

I will call
"A Current
Affair" and
ask them
how I can
order one.

When I am an old coot . . .

I WILL STROLL PROUDLY THROUGH THE MATERNITY WARD CARRYING A STUFFED BEAR AND PASSING OUT CIGARS.

I will engage telephone solicitors in endless conversation and discussion of my traumatic personal problems until **THEY HANG UP ON ME.**

When I am an old coot ...

I will go to baseball-card conventions.
I will put a big chew of tobacco in my
cheek and walk around spitting on the
floor and grabbing myself and claim to
HAVE PITCHED IN THE
1939 WORLD SERIES.

I will enroll
in junior
college and
argue with the
history teacher
when she gets
it wrong.

When I am an old coot . . .

I will write
to the
Preparation-H
company and
thank them
from the heart
of my bottom.

I will rent a gorilla suit
and wear it to the zoo

and jump out at people from behind
trees and grab their popcorn.

I WILL BUY A FISHING CABIN ON A RIVER AND FINANCE IT WITH A 30-YEAR MORTGAGE SO MY CHILDREN WILL REMEMBER ME WHEN I'M GONE.

I WILL DRIVE TO WEST
Texas for the fall foliage tour. Since
everyone else will be in New England
or the Rockies, there won't be much
traffic. Of course, there won't be
much foliage either.

When I am an old coot . . .

I will teach
my dog to fetch
my neighbor's
morning
newspaper, but
I will always
return it after
I have read
the sports
and comics.

I will petition the city council to return
the zoo animals to the wild and convert
the zoo into a jail so we can keep the
RIGHT CRITTERS LOCKED UP.

When I am an old coot . . .

I will watch all the old WESTERN MOVIES again. This time I will root for the Indians.

I WILL
HITCHHIKE
FROM TIME TO
TIME TO SEE
WHAT KIND
OF PERSON
WILL GIVE AN
OLD CODGER
A RIDE.

When I am an old coot . . .

I WILL ASSESS A

two-stroke penalty to any of my

old golfing partners who require

medical attention or have to relieve

themselves in the middle of a round.

I will tell the grandkids my TV is broken so they will have to listen to my stories.

When I am an old coot . . .

I WILL INVITE EVERY WOMAN I KNOW TO THE TOP OF THE EMPIRE STATE BUILDING AND ASK THEM IF WE EVER HAD "AN AFFAIR I CAN'T REMEMBER."

I will keep a
CAN OF EARTHWORMS
and a bucket of minnows
in my refrigerator.

When I am an old coot . . .

I will track down Willie Nelson and tell him I was wrong and he was right about some things.

I will let my
NOSE HAIR
grow so
I can
tickle my
sweetheart.

When I am an old coot . . .

I will drink cold milk from the jug and iced tea from the pitcher. I will eat blackberries from the vine, green onions from the ground, and peaches from the tree, but I WILL NOT EAT LIVER.

I will give all my stuff away. I
will not own anything that eats
(except for one old dog and a cat),

nor will I own anything
that is subject to government
inspection or property taxes.

When I am an old coot . . .

I WILL PREPARE A SPECIAL
dinner for myself every Friday night.
I will serve spaghetti with tomato sauce
and garlic bread. I will sip red wine and
sing along with Pavarotti and toast dear
friends, alive and dead.

I WILL
CALL ALL
POLITICIANS
WHO OPPOSE
PRAYER IN
SCHOOL AND
GIVE THEM A
GOOD CUSSING.

I will take my
pooper scooper
and transfer
the products of
my neighbor's
Great Dane
from my front
yard to the hood
of his Buick.

I WILL GET UP DURING THE NIGHT, SLIP ON MY NIKES, AND "JUST DO IT."

When I am an old coot . . .

I WILL INSIST ON
sitting on Santa's knee at the
department store, then throw a
squalling fit about the pony
I didn't get when I was six.

I will
spray air
freshener
around
old women
who smell
like flower
gardens.

When I am an old coot . . .

I will hide
bananas and
chocolate
brownies in my
sock drawer
and keep a
jar of peanut
butter under
my bed.

I WILL SMILE
SWEETLY AT
STRANGERS
AND OFFER TO
SHARE THE
PEPPERMINT
STICK THAT
I HAVE BEEN
LICKING.

When I am an old coot . . .

I will use my tweezers to poke bird
droppings into a cigarette

and wait for my worthless nephew
to bum a smoke again.

I will carry
a bottle of
Listerine to
my dentist's
office and
tell him I
will gargle
if he will.

When I am an old coot . . .

I WILL HANDCUFF MY WHEELCHAIR TO THE ICE-CREAM TRUCK UNTIL THE COMPANY AGREES TO MAKE TUTTI-FRUTTI AGAIN.

I will put a
Coke bottle in
my pants pocket
and tell my
nurse "it's the
real thing."

When I am an old coot . . .

I WILL APPEAR ON

Wheel of Fortune, and, when I solve

a puzzle, I will break down and

sobbingly confess that the game is

rigged and that Vanna gave me the

answer for half the loot.

I will sneak into the nursing home and slip Viagra into the mashed potatoes.

When I am an old coot . . .

I WILL CARRY MY PUTTER

wherever I go and use it as a cane,
back scratcher, and all-purpose
whacker. Sometimes I will flail
it around like Chi Chi Rodriguez.

I WILL HAVE POWER LUNCHES WITH MY CAT AT LONG JOHN SILVER'S.

When I am an old coot . . .

I WILL GROWL AT NERVOUS LITTLE DOGS IN PUBLIC PLACES AND MAKE THEM BARK FRANTICALLY.

I will
wrestle old,
worn-out
dogs and
pretend to
let them
pin me.

When I am an old coot . . .

I will disinherit my kids
★ ★ ★
and leave all my worldly possessions
to the lady who changes my covers
and gives me a bath.

I will dawdle
by the cleaning
lady, pretend
to stumble,
and grab her
buttocks firmly.

When I am an old coot ...

I WILL CAMP BENEATH

the stars in City Park and eat beans from

a can and chew tobacco. I will sing "Home

on the Range" and pee on the smoldering

campfire to make it sizzle.

I WILL
PROCURE
A WHITE
JACKET AND
STETHOSCOPE
AND ROAM
THE HALLS OF
THE HOSPITAL
ACTING
IMPORTANT.

I will attend public meetings and raise hell with officials about whatever is on the agenda.

I will break
wind in
public
places
and frown
disgustedly
at the fellow
beside me.

When I am an old coot . . .

I WILL ATTEND FANCY

art auctions, sip champagne and munch

little watercress sandwiches, and bid on

van Goghs and Picassos. Then, if I am

the high bidder, I will blame it on my

dandruff and itchy scalp.

I WILL SMOKE
RUM CROOK
CIGARS IN
AIRLINE
LAVATORIES
AND DARE
THE FLIGHT
ATTENDANT TO
THROW ME OFF
THE PLANE.

When I am an old coot . . .

Every Columbus
Day I will
walk around
the courthouse
with a sign that
says "Indians
Discovered
America."

I will fake an asthma
attack and break into
A FIT OF LOUD COUGHING
when the preacher talks too long and
the Cowboys have a noon kickoff on **TV.**

When I am an old coot ...

I WILL SEND FLOWERS

and candy to myself and display them before my friends at The Home. They will come with little cards signed by such dear friends as Hillary, Oprah, and Dolly.

I WILL WRITE
LETTERS TO
THE EDITOR
EXTOLLING
THE JOYS
AND SOCIAL
BENEFITS OF
PROSTITUTION
AND SIGN
THE MAYOR'S
NAME.

I will teach
the children
to belch
"Clementine"
when their
mommies are
not around.

I will stroll around Graceland
in a white jumpsuit
★ ★ ★
and introduce myself as Elvis's uncle.

When I am an old coot . . .

I WILL PRETEND TO BE AN INSPECTOR FROM THE WILDLIFE COMMISSION AND GO FISHING AT THE HATCHERY.

I will go to confession and make up wild stories about the local parishioners and never admit to being a Presbyterian.

When I am an old coot . . .

I will crow like a rooster at sunrise and whenever else the mood strikes me.

I WILL GO
BOWLING AND
PLAY POKER
WITH THE
BOYS AND
EAT PRUNES
AND BE A
REGULAR GUY.

I will hook
a pair of
Huskies to my
wheelchair
and pretend
to be Charlton
Heston.

I will safety-pin my socks
together when I wash them
so the blue ones and black ones
DON'T TRY TO MATE.

I WILL DROP MY DENTURES INTO THE PUNCH BOWL AT PARTIES WHEN I THINK THE OTHERS HAVE HAD ENOUGH.

I will
butter my
pills so they
don't get
hung in my
esophagus.

When I am an old coot . . .

I will lobby the legislature for a
sin tax on ice cream and donuts.
They have done me more harm
THAN CIGARETTES
AND WHISKEY.

I will teach the children not to gamble

by cheating them in little card games
and taking their lunch money.

When I am an old coot . . .

I WILL RESCUE BIRD-DOGS FROM THOSE TINY LITTLE CAGES.

I will file a complaint against my proctologist for trespassing and unlawful entry.

When I am an old coot . . .

I will rig
up a little
bungee
jump for my
neighbor's
yelping
Chihuahua.

I WILL
PIERCE MY
NOSTRIL AND
ENTERTAIN
THE CHILDREN
BY BLOWING
MY NOSE LIKE
A WHALE.

When I am an old coot . . .

I will take
steam baths
and stroll
naked around
the locker
room and hang
out with my
buddies.

I WILL TRICK MY FRIENDS

at The Home by standing at the door and collecting a small admission for various little programs the church presents.

When I am an old coot . . .

I will carry a bucket of paint in
the back of my pickup truck

and create handicap-parking spaces
wherever I think they should be.

I WILL PUT
EXPENSIVE
PRICE TAGS ON
CHEAP GIFTS
AND PRETEND
THAT I FORGOT
TO TAKE
THEM OFF.

When I am an old coot . . .

I WILL SHOW UP AT
wedding receptions and stuff
myself with fancy hors d'oeuvres
and whisper nasty little comments
about the groom's family secrets.

I will ask
people for
directions
and then
argue with
them.

When I am an old coot . . .

I will tell all my family members
that, for my next birthday,
I WOULD LIKE TO RECEIVE CASH
instead of socks and ties.

I will promptly
return the
handkerchiefs
that I borrow
to clean my
ears and blow
my nose.

When I am an old coot . . .

I will join the volunteer fire department
and put emergency lights
and a siren on my pickup truck.

I will use them often to make sure
they are working properly.

I WILL CARRY A LITTLE WHISK BROOM AND BRUSH THE DANDRUFF FROM PEOPLE'S SHOULDERS.

When I am an old coot . . .

I will save
my used
dental floss
to tie bows
and name
tags on
little gifts.

I will invite David Letterman's mama to cover the "Old Coot Winter Olympics" in Miami.

When I am an old coot . . .

I WILL CARRY
DRIED DOG AND
CAT FOOD IN
THE BACK OF
MY TRUCK FOR
OLD STRAYS
THAT I COME
ACROSS.

I WILL OCCASIONALLY

ride a broomstick to breakfast and

insist that the cafeteria lady bring

an extra bowl of oats for my horse.

When I am an old coot . . .

I will write the Quarter Horse
Association and nominate the
electric company as "Stud of the Year"
for the way it services its customers.

I will go to the Gourmet Room at the Ritz-Carlton and order a pitcher of buttermilk and half a cantaloupe full of chili.

When I am an old coot ...

I will sit in the
Little League
stands and yell
instructions
to every coach
and player
on the field.

I WILL GET
DOWN ON MY
KNEES FROM
TIME TO TIME
AND TRY TO
SNEAK UP
ON OLD DOGS,
GRANDKIDS,
BROOK TROUT,
AND THE
GOOD LORD.

When I am an old coot ...

I will stand up at the Sportsmen's
Banquet and announce that the best way
TO HAVE "DUCKS UNLIMITED"
is to stop shooting their butts off.

I WILL GET OUT
MY OLD SCHOOL
PICTURES AND
TOAST THE
MEMORY OF
MRS. MAY, MY
THIRD-GRADE
TEACHER,
AND TELL
HER I STILL
LOVE HER.

When I am an old coot . . .

I WILL DANCE WITH MY
wife in the kitchen and nibble her ear
and make her giggle. I will write little
poems for her and thank her for being
a saint and a soldier.

I will
introduce my
grandchildren
to the rhythm
and blues
of Lightnin'
Hopkins and
Jimmy Reed.

When I am an old coot ...

I will carry a styrofoam cooler

with artichokes, anchovies,

jalapeños, and Grey Poupon to add

ZEST TO FAST FOODS.

I will also carry a bottle of Maalox.

I will learn to play the harmonica like a freight train and make up hobo stories about riding the rails with Boxcar Willie.

When I am an old coot . . .

I will reserve
a window seat
on the flight
into Dulles
International
and moon
Congress from
40,000 feet.

I WILL BORROW
A BAILIFF'S
UNIFORM
AND FRISK
PROSPECTIVE
JURORS AS
THEY ARRIVE
AT THE
COURTHOUSE.

When I am an old coot . . .

I WILL CALL
THAT TV
PREACHER
WHO HUSTLES
EVERYBODY
AND TELL HIM
MY PRAYER
REQUEST
IS THAT
HE GET AN
HONEST JOB.

I will carry
toothpicks for
friends who
occasionally
have green
vegetables
hanging from
their teeth.

When I am an old coot . . .

I will paint
my golf
balls bright
chartreuse
to match
my pants.

I WILL
DEMONSTRATE
MY DEXTERITY
AND STEADY
HAND BY
EATING PEAS
WITH A TABLE
KNIFE.

When I am an old coot . . .

I WILL POLICE
the express check-out line at the
supermarket and deny entry to
anyone with more than ten items.

I will hop
on my
snowmobile
and
"kick ice"
across the
mountain.

When I am an old coot . . .

I will stroll through the cemetery singing, "I've got friends in low places."

I will eat blue-corn tortillas and refried beans and sit by the campfire and sing, "You are the wind beneath my jeans."

When I am an old coot . . .

I WILL GO TO THE SUPER
Bowl and slip onto the field at halftime
and play my trombone with the marching
band on national TV. I will spend the
second half of the game in jail.

I WILL KNIT
MICHAEL
JACKSON
ANOTHER
GLOVE SO HE
WON'T KEEP
SHIVERING
AND GRABBING
HIMSELF TO
GET WARM.

When I am an old coot . . .

I will call
life insurance
salesmen at
home and ask
them why they
don't bug me
anymore.

I will carry a black robe and Bible

and administer the wedding vows to any
couple who appears to need marrying.

When I am an old coot . . .

I WILL STAND
ON A PHONE
BOOK AT
GIRLIE SHOWS
IN CASE I
WANT TO
REACH OUT
AND TOUCH
SOMEONE.

I WILL TEST THE PATIENCE

of my golfing partners by taking little
naps while frozen over important putts.

I will go to
Billy Bob's
Honky-Tonk
and have that
shoe-shine
cowgirl shine
the dance back
into my boots.

I WILL SAVE A LOT OF MONEY ON BARBERS.

When I am an old coot . . .

I will take a trailer of young farm
animals to the inner-city park

and give every kid the chance to ride a
pony, pet a rabbit, and scratch a pig's ear.

I WILL
OPEN THE
POLYESTER
WAX MUSEUM
AT THE HOME
AND GET MY
DOMINO PALS
TO HOLD A
POSE WHEN
PAYING
CUSTOMERS
ARRIVE.

When I am an old coot...

I will refuse
to grow old
gracefully and
will leave this
world like I
came in—

★ ★ ★

kicking,
squalling, and
raising a stink.

I will ask
my young
nurse if
she would
like to
jump-start
my
pacemaker.

When I am an old coot . . .

I WILL RECRUIT MY

friends in rockers and wheelchairs and

form a rock 'n' roll band. We will call

our group "The Rolling Kidney Stones."

Our fans will be called "Cooties."

I WILL GIVE
THE LITTLE
LADIES AT THE
HOME A THRILL
BY ASKING
IF THEY
WOULD LIKE
TO GO STEADY
AND SWAP
DENTURES.

When I am an old coot . . .

I will distribute hammers to residents
at The Home so they can open
those little tamper-proof pill bottles
THEIR MEDICINE COMES IN.

I will
double up
on the Old
Spice when
I haven't
showered
for a few
days.

When I am an old coot . . .

I WILL BURN MY

Christmas lights all year, put a

jack-o'-lantern in my window,

and erect an eight-foot Easter

bunny in the front yard beside

my cardboard Clint Eastwood.

I WILL ATTEND WEDDING RECEPTIONS AND LICK THE KNIFE FOR GOOD LUCK BEFORE THE BRIDE AND GROOM CUT THE CAKE.

When I am an old coot . . .

I WILL WEAR TWO NECKTIES ON SPECIAL OCCASIONS.

I will slip an
Alka Seltzer
inside my cheek
and tell the
nurse I think I
have rabies.

I WILL STOP SEARCHING AND PROCLAIM THAT I HAVE FOUND MYSELF, AND I AM PRETTY SILLY.

I WILL GO TO ANTIQUE AUCTIONS AND TRY TO SELL MY BODY.

When I am an old coot . . .

I will take my bedroll to the
Farmers Market and curl up in the
fragrant shade of a load of ripe
cantaloupes and let my nose
TAKE ME BACK TO GRANDPA.

I will practice "Cootspa" to get my way:

★ ★ ★

from outrageous charm to cantankerous intimidation.

When I am an old coot . . .

I WILL TAKE
LITTLE TRIPS
INSIDE MY
HEAD AND
VISIT WITH
DEPARTED
FRIENDS. I
WILL DANCE
WITH ANGELS
WHENEVER
I HEAR THE
MUSIC.